(TRANSPORT)

— 21

Royalty on the Road

Lord Montagu of Beaulieu

With Michael Frostick
Foreword by H.R.H. Prince Michael of Kent

Collins
St James's Place, London
1980

FRONTISPIECE:
Nicholas II, last Czar of all the Russias,
inspects his troops c 1914.
The car is a Delaunay-Belleville.

William Collins Sons & Co Ltd
London · Glasgow · Sydney · Auckland
Toronto · Johannesburg

First published 1980
© *Lord Montagu of Beaulieu*
ISBN 0 00 221694 4
Set in Monophoto Photina
Filmset and Printed in Great Britain by
BAS Printers Limited, Over Wallop, Hampshire

Contents

———————

Acknowledgements

Her Majesty The Queen
Her Majesty Queen Mary
His Majesty King Michael of Rumania
His Royal Highness the Duke of Kent
His Excellency the Egyptian Ambassador
Baron E. de Graffenried
Major BEM T. de Maere d'Aertrycke, Le Commandant des Palais Royaux, Brussels
Signor Tito Anselmi
Dr. Asok Kumar Das, MA. LL.B, PH.D, Director, Maharaja Sawai Man Singh II Museum, Jaipur
S.B. Debnam Esq
Ms Jean Denton
G.V. Eyles Esq
Michael Frostick Esq
G.N. Georgano Esq, MA., Head Librarian, National Motor Museum
Heinrich Goldhahn Esq. Automobil Veteranen Club of Austria
Lt. Col. P.H. Hasslett
A. Hendry Esq
Miss E. Palmstierna, Comptroller of the Household of His Royal Highness Prince Bertil of Sweden
Ronald Priestley Esq
Roland Pym Esq
Bunty Scott-Moncrieff Esq
Herr Juggmann, Sekretariat Schloss Salem, Germany
Paul van Leewen Esq
A.E. Ulmann Esq
Archive Neuhaus
Centro Storico Fiat
Country Life
News Editor, The Hindu, Madras
Imperial War Museum
Mercedes Benz Bildarchiv
Museo Biscaretti
Norsk Teknisk Museum
Radio Times, Hulton Picture Library
Slottets Bibliotek, Norway
Ullstein G.M.B.H. Bilderdienst, Berlin
Vauxhall Motors Limited

Foreword

The heroines of Lord Montagu's comprehensive and delightfully absorbing collection of motoring photographs are surely the Rolls-Royces and Daimlers. Other motor-cars, he suggests, were and are faster, more dashing and perhaps more fun to drive, but Rolls-Royces and Daimlers have successfully withstood the competition of the world's other great car builders.

I am delighted and proud that members of the British royal family have played a worthwhile part in the development of motoring, motor-racing and motor-cars over the last ninety years. My own motoring, at the end of that time, has been fast, varied and exhilarating.

Sadly, Lord Montagu predicts that the end of elegant royal motoring—indeed of all motoring—cannot be far off. If he is right, and I sincerely hope that he is mistaken, this book will be a unique portrait of one aspect of our age: the age of the motor-car.

If, however, we are in for a brighter motoring future, this book will be a most valuable dictionary of excitement, danger, elegance, engineering attainment and virtuosity for those who follow on.

Michael

Part One

From the Beginning

1898–1918

*F*or all that the piston engine was a Victorian invention, we never hear anyone talk of a Victorian car. The good Queen was, of course, a very old lady by the time cars appeared on the road; and she was not keen on change. According to Lytton Strachey the industrial developments of her reign meant little to her, and left her 'perfectly cold'. Since the early motorists were the young, the rich and the fashionable, no doubt Her Majesty expressed her disapproval of cars to 'Bertie', the Prince of Wales. But as she expressed little to him *other* than disapproval she probably succeeded only in stimulating his interest in the things.

There is some doubt as to when the Prince of Wales took his first drive in a motor-car. It is frequently said to have been with John Scott Montagu, the author's father, in the New Forest in August 1899; although there is evidence that he went on a short outing from Warwick Castle in a six horse-power Daimler in June 1898, and another school of thought claims that the Prince 'first tried a motor-car' at an exhibition in South Kensington.

The New Forest adventure happened while the Prince was staying at Highcliffe Castle near Christchurch. One day when John Scott Montagu had been invited over to lunch it was suggested that the Royal party might like to take a drive in his Daimler. The proud owner at the wheel, the Prince beside him, and two ladies of the party in the back seats, they travelled seven or eight miles up the Lyndhurst–Southampton road and back.

The well known photograph which appears on the jacket of this book was taken just after that run. The Prince questioned his 'chauffeur' closely as to what sort of vehicle would be suitable for his own use, and commented to the windswept ladies in the back of the car that such devices would surely change the prevailing fashion in big hats. A few weeks later Montagu was summoned to Marlborough House and asked to bring his Daimler along. It remained there for a week while interested parties—no doubt influenced by associations with Daimler—examined it. As a result of that visit an order was placed for the first royal Daimler.

When the Prince became King Edward VII he made two more visits to Beaulieu, and on both occasions went out in the car with his host. The trips were not without incident. There is a tale of a gatekeeper at Lymington toll bridge who was not at all impressed on being told to hurry up as the King was in the car. 'I know them kings,' he said, 'one of 'em slipped past me only this morning! Pay yer sixpence first, and then you can wait till I've let this donkey cart through.'

In fact these first royal trips were of great importance to the motoring movement—and to the industry that was to grow from it; for cars had many die-hard opponents, and the royal interest, added to the fact that in April 1902 a reigning English monarch had been driven in a car and subsequently bought one himself, were important factors in getting the new invention accepted.

Certain Continental monarchs had a very great influence on the development of the motor car—among them Leopold, King of the Belgians. From the earliest times car bodies had tended to resemble horse-drawn carriages—the entrance to the back seats often being from the rear, as in a dog cart. This did not make for either comfort or elegance. The story goes that one evening the Belgian king was discussing the shape of his new car with a lady of his acquaintance, Cléo de Mérode—an actress and dancer. Miss Mérode, tired of scrambling into the back of the existing models, pushed a small sofa and two armchairs together in the middle of her boudoir, to represent the seats of a car. With a wave of the hand she then indicated where the doors should be, thus designing not only the King's new car, but all the cars that came after it. The King wisely had the design implemented and took the credit for it; but next time you get into a car spare a thought for that clever woman.

In quite a different way His Most Catholic Majesty King Alfonso XIII of Spain influenced early motoring. He was an out and out enthusiast; he drove fast and well every model of every car he could lay his hands on, and even gave his name to one of the early and very successful Hispano-Suiza models—the 'Alfonso'. In this case royal patronage was a boon to the manufacturer and to the country's industry. The Italian industry was similarly stimulated when in 1907 Prince Borghese competed in what was perhaps the wildest event in motoring history—the Pekin to Paris Race. The Prince won it, driving an Itala.

The series of motoring events organized by the Kaiser's brother, Prince Henry of Prussia—the Prince Henry Tours—aroused interest all over Europe. The third event was won by young Ferdinand Porsche in an Austro Daimler of his design—thus anticipating the important part he was to play in the development of the European car. The fourth event took place in Great Britain, where a number of stately homes, including the author's home, Beaulieu, were visited. Vauxhall had some success in these races and one of their models—the first car ever to be advertised as a 'sports car'—was called the 'Prince Henry'.

Of course motoring in those early days involved hazards to which even royalty, when it took to the road, was exposed. One day when the author's father was travelling down to Bucklers Hard in his twelve horse-power Daimler it suddenly swung into a ditch, throwing his wife out. When the car was examined it was found that there was a fault in the steering due to a weak part. Realizing that His Majesty had just purchased an exactly similar model, Montagu immediately telegraphed a warning to Marlborough House. The royal car was inspected, and the same fault found. The manufacturers, of course, put matters right at once, but it is not difficult to imagine how much harm would have been done to the whole cause of motoring if the King had been involved in an accident.

The Paris–Madrid race of 1903 was stopped at Bordeaux by the French government because of the great number of accidents that had occurred to both drivers and spectators. The cars were not allowed to motor even to the railway station, but had to be towed there by horses before being returned to Paris by train. This led to closed-circuit racing, in which Great Britain was at a disadvantage, since it was illegal to close public roads in Britain for racing. There was a famous series of races for the Gordon Bennett Cup in which some curious nationalistic regulations lifted their comic heads. A German car, for example, was supposed to be wholly German, so that it could be disqualified if the leather on the seats had not come from German cows. When it was Britain's turn to host the event it had to be run in Ireland where the law was more flexible. The French got a bit fed up with this, and started a series of Grands Prix in which they felt they had a better chance; and motor-racing in Britain might well have come to an end had not Mr and Mrs Locke-King built a circuit on some ground they had at Weybridge, known as Brooklands, in 1907.

Ever since the days of the steam coach, and certainly in the first ten years of the motor-car's existence, driving in Britain had been fiercely controlled by law. Successive acts had demanded that at least three men be employed to drive a 'locomotive'—and that one of them walk in front with a red flag. There was a speed limit of four miles per hour; a ten-pound licence fee had to be paid for in every county in which the locomotive was used; and no bridge might be crossed unless it sported a notice saying so. With the new 'Emancipation' Act of 1896 there was much more freedom. It abolished the man walking in front, allowed for only one man to drive the car, and raised the speed limit from four to twelve miles per hour.

Eventually, in 1905, the Automobile Association came into being to fight the motorist's cause, and the Royal Automobile Club (founded in 1897) existed to prove royal patronage if nothing else. However, there was still a more or less permanent state of war between motorists and the police. Such a state of affairs made it difficult for members of the royal family to drive themselves, as a clash with the police on any matter was to be avoided; and indeed to a lesser extent this problem still exists today.

In 1896, the same year as the new Act, a second Motor Show was held in Great Britain—this time at the Imperial Institute—and was attended by the Prince of Wales. Because of the adverse legislation there had been virtually no British motor industry up to this time, and the French and Germans had had things all their own way; but now things were to be different. With the change in the law British businessmen saw the possibilities in motor manufacturing. Led by H. J. Lawson, who bought the Daimler patent rights for England—and a huge disused cotton mill in Coventry—they began to produce the first recognizably British cars.

Compared to many other inventions the car grew up quickly and by 1910 had become an everyday sight. Still only really available to the rich, it was nevertheless reliable and comfortable. Electric lighting had arrived and was fitted to the Daimlers ordered for the British royal family in that year. The design of their coachwork remained almost unchanged until about 1953. For all those years, although bonnets grew longer and drivers were eventually enclosed, the basic shape remained—a royal Daimler was a royal Daimler.

Further afield designs were a good deal more exotic, and nowhere more so than in Imperial Russia. The British Lagonda company (founded by an American who came to London with the intention of being an opera singer and stayed to become a motor manufacturer) had considerable success in Russia, with models they never offered for sale in the rest of Europe. The Czar himself, however, had his own preference, and it was for the French make Delaunay-Belleville. This company was primarily famous for its railway locomotives and steamship boilers—many of which were supplied to Russia's navy. They also made massive and magnificent motor-cars—with round radiators and bonnets so that no one should forget their steam origins. These were the royal cars of Russia. Delaunay-Belleville went so far as to make one special (and immense) model called the SMT (*Sa Majesté le Tsar*).

When Princess Alice of Battenberg and Prince Andreas of Greece (the parents of Prince Philip) were married at Darmstadt in October 1903 their wedding present from the Czar was a British Wolseley, with what must have been one of the first 'hard tops' ever made. The *Car Illustrated* of the time says: 'It is at once a handsome and eminently serviceable vehicle. There is seating for five passengers and the driver, and the general arrangements are very well carried out with regard to comfort and utility. For inclement weather the omnibus top is most effective. It is readily detachable and a separate canopy is provided for fine weather.'

By 1914 the car was technically more or less adult. Of course developments in metallurgy, rubber and plastic were still to come, and the early motorist, whether royal or commoner, did—perfectly well—without accessories such as windscreen wipers, radios and cigar lighters. As war approached the royal cars were pressed into military service: Rolls-Royces became armoured and Vauxhall plunged into the business of making 'staff cars'.

There were already signs that governments everywhere, and in Great Britain Lloyd George in particular, saw the newly developing motor cars as a kind of 'Milch Cow' for their failing finances. Roads which had started as little more than tracks now developed acceptable surfaces; a motor-driven cab could be had in London for the effort of waving an umbrella; and the motor-bus was upon us. The same was true of Paris, Berlin and every other 'civilized' capital. The century of the motor-car was under way, and the royal families of the world were giving it their full support.

Although controversy rages as to exactly when and where he took to the road,
the first British royal motorist was undoubtedly Edward VII, and his
first drive is generally agreed to have been at Warwick Castle on 25 June 1898,
when he was Prince of Wales. Some authorities say he was taken
'up the road and back' by the Hon. Evelyn Ellis at the motor exhibition
at the Imperial Institute in 1896; others claim that his first real outing
was when driven in a Daimler by the author's father in 1899.
Here, from a society journal of the day, is an artist's impression of
the Warwick Castle drive. The car is a twin-cylinder Daimler.

Though deliberately similar, these two photographs are separated by some eighty years.
The first was taken after John Scott-Montagu had driven the Prince of Wales
on his first long motor trip. The occasion arose when His Royal Highness was staying
at Highcliffe, near Christchurch, and the author's father was invited over to lunch.
He went in his new 12 horse-power Daimler and in the afternoon took the Prince of Wales
and two female members of the houseparty out for a run in the New Forest.
It was on their return to Highcliffe that a local schoolmaster took the picture.

The Montagu car had a distinguished history in its own right, being the first ever
to make an authorized entry into the Yard of the Houses of Parliament.
It had also taken third place in the Tourist Class of the 1899 Paris-Ostend Race.
As it is still at Beaulieu and now fully restored, it seemed natural to ask Prince Charles
on a recent visit if he would pose with the author in the place previously occupied
by his great-great-grandfather. He was graciously pleased to do so, and managed
to look as quizzically interested in this sort of thing as had his forbear.

Queen Mary
(Victoria Mary, Duchess of York as she then was) driven by the Hon. C. S. Rolls
(the Rolls of Rolls-Royce) in one of his own cars, with Lady Llangattock,
his mother and Lady Eva Dugdale. 'My first drive in a motor—
to visit Raglan etc.' wrote the Duchess in her diary.

28 May 1902: His Majesty King Edward VII in a 24 horse-power Daimler driven by John Scott-Montagu. This was His Majesty's first motor outing after he became King; but it was still before the coronation (which had to be put off while the royal appendix was removed).

Queen Mary, then Princess of Wales, at the wheel of a Panhard in 1903.
The Prince, later George V, is sitting at the very back of the car.
There seems to be no record of Queen Mary ever having driven herself,
which may account for the slightly amused expression she is wearing.
One has to remember that at this time the car was still a new toy
and often formed the setting for photographs.

The original caption reads: 'Four royal automobilists at Sandringham';
all that is missing is the car. From left to right the adults are:
King Edward VII, the Kaiser, the Queen, the Prince of Wales (later George V) and Princess Victoria.
The children are: Princess Mary, Prince Albert (later George VI), Prince Henry (later Duke of Gloucester)
and Prince Edward (later Edward VIII).

With a gently possessive hand on the wheel—
a pose often adopted for photographs by those who did not drive—
H.R.H. the Duke of Connaught in a two-cylinder Napier.
The chauffeur standing in front of the car is holding
what looks like a bulb horn with which to give, on command,
'audible warning of approach'. On second thoughts
it might well be a starting handle!

Thanks to a distinguished racing career, Napier was
the pre-eminent British make in the first years of the century.
The cars did not, however, attract royal patronage
to the same extent as the Daimlers.

The Duke of Connaught (he is in the back on the right)—
this time with 'other officers' and a chauffeur in place.
The real charm of the picture is in the attitude of the soldier with
the second car, oblivious of the fact that everyone else in sight
is standing stiffly to attention. The car is a 10 horse-power Wolseley
with a two-cylinder engine, then Britain's best-selling car.
Its designer was Herbert Austin, who would set up on his own in 1905.

———————————

A mysterious picture dating from about 1905
The gentleman 'en chapeau melon' (bowler hat) is King Albert of the Belgians,
and the small boy standing on the axle is the future King Leopold.
The car would appear to be a Darracq. The event has not been identified.

The Czar of all the Russias on manoeuvres in about 1905.
With him are the Empress and Prince N. V. Orlov.
The car is a Delaunay-Belleville—the early four-cylinder species.
Later the Czar's garages would house a fine selection of
this expensive French make. A special 70 horse-power six-cylinder series,
the SMT (for Sa Majesté Le Tsar) was an Imperial exclusive.

Although the First World War
was still some way off, here is
Victor Emannuel III of Italy
on manoeuvres in 1907.
The car is a 24/40 horse-power Fiat:
in those days the famous Torinese firm
was still concentrating on
expensive luxury cars with close
affinities to the German Mercedes.
The chauffeur's long motoring coat,
which now looks so unusual,
was common wear at the time—
it served as a kind of overall.

Infante Alfonso de Orleans-Bourbon, son of King Alfonso XIII of Spain,
in about 1908 driving a Gobron-Brillié while a student at Heidelberg.
Gobron-Brilliés featured complex opposed-piston engines (two pistons per cylinder)
though in other respects they were conventional, with the side-chain drive favoured
on big cars of the period. This one is probably the 60 horse-power 7.6-litre four.

Prince Alfonso again at the wheel of a very early Minerva in or around 1905.
Belgium's most famous make had yet to acquire its classical radiator shape
or goddess mascot, and the earliest models were far from luxury machines.

Princess Alexandra of Hohenlohe-Langenberg
(daughter of the Duke of Edinburgh
who was one of Queen Victoria's sons and
later became the Duke of Saxe-Coburg-Gotha)
at the wheel of the family's first car—
a Daimler (Mercedes) from Stuttgart.

One of the splendid Delaunay-Bellevilles that belonged to the Russian royal house.
This is certainly a six-cylinder, possibly an 8-litre O-type of 1913–4.
Note the wide rear rims and twin rear tyres.

'Nicholas II, Emperor of Russia,' says the original caption.
Everyone at the salute, including the seated chauffeur, and winter conditions
not being allowed to interfere with royal motoring. Note in this, and in other pictures
from Russia, the huge lamps with which all that country's cars were equipped.

———————————

*The little Wolseley which the Czar gave to Princess Alice of Battenburg
(Prince Philip's mother) when she married Prince Andreas of Greece.
It has a 'de-mountable' saloon to the rear which can be used as an open car
or with the Surrey on top.* Car Illustrated *said at the time:
'in inclement weather the omnibus top is most effective'.
This is another example of the horizontal-twin which sold so well
in the* 1902–4 *period.*

THE KAISER AT THE PRIORY

*The Kaiser on a state visit to Great Britain in 1907
was driven in this Daimler by Mr H. G. Debnam,
and is seen here at Christchurch Priory.*

The Kaiser talking informally between two of the official Mercedes cars—note the crowns on the lamps. Time and place unknown, but the cars appear to be of 1910–2 vintage.

The Kaiser transfers from a royal Mercedes to a royal horse.
Date and place again unknown. Since its introduction in 1901, Germany's
Mercedes had become the pre-eminent car of Europe's royalty and aristocracy,
even if over the ensuing decade its 'revolutionary' features
(pressed-steel frame, honeycomb radiator, selective gate gearchange)
had won wholesale acceptance.

*Prince Ludwig of Bavaria was
often seen at the wheel of a car
and this picture shows him on a visit
to some local factories.
Neither the make of the car nor
the names of the other occupants
are known.*

The royal princesses of Luxembourg take an outing by motor.
From left to right they are Princess Marie-Adelaide,
Princess Hilda, Princess Antonia and Princess Charlotte.
No date is put upon the event; but it would seem
to be after Cleo de Mérode had told the king
of neighbouring Belgium what shape a car body should be.

Prince Max of Baden (grandfather of the present Margrave)
with his driver Mr Baumert.
The entire staff of the Gasthaus is obviously
intrigued by the Prince's splendid new Benz.

The King of Siam at the wheel of one of his early cars,
this one sporting a magnificent mascot and special shielded headlights.
The first royal car in Siam was driven by steam,
but this was not a great success and subsequent models were
mostly more conventional ones manufactured by Daimler-Benz
and then given long Siamese names.
Cars played a great part in the life of the royal household:
even the queen and the princesses learned to drive.

T.R.H. The Prince of Wales & Prince Albert at Headland Hotel

Their youthful Royal Highnesses, the Prince of Wales and Prince Albert,
taking quite naturally to the motor-car.
The car is probably a Thornycroft, product of the famous
British marine engineers who also built commercial vehicles.
After 1913 they concentrated on these latter.
This photograph was used as an advertisement by the hotel in Newquay.

———————————

King Victor Emannuel III
driving an electric car in 1904.

A miniature Cadillac specially designed in 1912 and given by
Queen Alexandra to her nephew Crown Prince Olaf of Norway.
It looks like the contemporary four-cylinder 30, produced
in various forms from 1905 until 1914, and was powered by
the then newly introduced Cadillac Electric starter.
It is now carefully preserved in the technical museum at Oslo.

King George V started his wheeled career in a simpler,
but at the time even more fashionable manner.

George V in 1909 with a 'shooting brake'
which he had had made on a Daimler chassis—
a forerunner of today's estate cars.
This car appears to be a fairly new one;
it was, however, common aristocratic practice
to 'demote' a discarded formal carriage,
and rebody it for the butts!

A wonderfully Edwardian scene:
Edward VII in Algeria in 1905, with
the Hon. Harry Stonor second from left,
and Frederick Ponsonby holding a
check cap in his hand.

A group outside York Cottage, Sandringham, with Edward VII at the wheel.
He was a confirmed motorist by this time.
Queen Alexandra stands by the front wheel in a dark costume
with a muff; George V, then Prince of Wales, sits on the front
of the car with Princess Victoria (Queen Mary) behind him.
Though we can barely see it the car is almost certainly a Daimler.

1904: 'Edward VII about to enter his Daimler car'.
This would have been one of a succession of
chain-driven side-valve fours which were made in
a great diversity of models in the 1904–8 period.
With lighter bodywork they were excellent performers, and had
a distinguished record in sprints and hillclimbs.

H.M. KING EDWARD VII about to enter his DAIMLER CAR.

The Kaiser on manoeuvres in 1908.
The Imperial Rainbow which has been
superimposed on the picture
is not explained.

The Kaiser takes his first ride.
Military uniform was more or less inevitable—
and the car, of course, is a Daimler; but from
a different factory from the British ones.
The year is 1903.

Edward VII visits the Kaiser at Homburg in 1906. The car is a very special Mercedes Simplex which had an enormous glass screen behind the chauffeur. Note that chain drive still features on this make: it was used on some of the sporting models as late as 1914. The second picture shows the two monarchs in a particularly cheerful mood with their ladies well wrapped up against those dusty roads.

Minor royalty was much given to being photographed in its motors.
Not having to worry about actually driving the car, Princess Carlotta
of Sachesen-Meiningen looks charming with her new N.A.G. in 1909.

The Grand Duke of Mecklenburg-Schwerin at the wheel of his Mercedes,
complete with picnic basket.

*Queen Margherita of Savoy had this Landaulette built for her by the famous
Italian coachbuilder Cesare Sala on a 24/40 horse-power Fiat chassis in 1906 or 1907.
The 'Mercedes look'—and a Mercedes-like technical specification—would linger
into 1910 on the bigger Fiats. This particular car has coronets on the coach-lamps
and an unusually early St Christopher mascot on the radiator cap.
The Queen's use of this mascot is said to have popularized St Christopher
as the patron saint of motorists.*

Surely the most magnificent of tourers.
It was built for Queen Margherita by Messrs C. Castagna,
an old-established firm of coach-makers in Milan
which had recently gone over to motor cars.
The lighting arrangements are almost unbelievable
in their magnificence and there is a clock
set into the rear door.
Castagna, of course, would later become famous
for elegant bodywork (not always formal)
on Isotta Fraschini and Alfa Romeo chassis
in the inter-war period.

The Ehrhardt, an ancestor of the present B.M.W.,
was one of the cars which came from the Dixi factory.
Here, visiting the Dixi works at Eisenach in 1904,
is the Grand Duke of Saxe-Weimar-Eisenach.

1906: Victor Emannuel III of Italy
in an open car built on a Fiat 24/40 horse-power chassis.

*One of the men who put royalty in front on the road was Prince Henry of Prussia,
the Kaiser's brother, seen here competing in the Herkomer trial in 1906.
He was not only an enthusiastic and successful driver himself, but was also
the founder of the Prince Henry Trials, after which several famous cars,
a Vauxhall for example, were named*

The official Prince Henry autograph photograph—
complete with the familiar overall motoring coat.
And a good advertisement for Benz, who probably sponsored it,
since their name on the bonnet is so carefully retouched!

When it came to the Prince Henry trials
the prince was no mere sponsor, pleased to lend his name
from regal heights, but was actively concerned with every aspect of the event.
He is seen here talking to Fritz Erle
of the Benz team in Vienna at the start of the 1909 event.
The car in the centre (no. 627) is, however, an Opel, then still a fairly
expensive make, and one favoured by the House of Hesse.

Prince Henry takes delivery of a new Benz —
a big four-cylinder model of the type
which replaced the primitive belt-driven Velos.
These were, however, still current
as late as 1902.

The other great European motoring monarch was King Alfonso XIII of Spain.
He appears here in a new six-cylinder Hispano-Suiza
in which he had been driving at speeds of up to 75 m.p.h.
—quite something in those days!

The most famous of all Hispanos—the one to which His Majesty gave his name.
The 'Alfonso' Hispano is a motoring legend. This one appears to be
a standard roadster offering over 70 m.p.h. (and 25 m.p.g.) from a mere 3·6 litres.
The King is shown here in 1913 taking part in a parade in honour
of Monsieur Poincaré, President of France.

King Alfonso in 1914 in a British Daimler with Spanish coachwork.
By now Daimler had switched to the Silent Knight sleeve-valve engine and worm drive.
Style changed little for many years, so this one could be almost any of the
mid-range types from the 25 horse-power four to the 38 horse-power six.
For once His Majesty is not at the wheel, but 'in the middle' again.

This enthusiastic royal motorist is Prince Wilhelm of Sweden,
seen at the wheel of a Benz in about 1913 (the car is a 1910/1 model).
After the war he had a Bugatti which was never registered in Sweden,
but kept for his use in France.

*When royalty did not choose a Daimler
the German Benz was the obvious alternative.
This car, dating from about 1908,
belonged to the Swedish royal house.
Once again it has coronets on the lamps
and on the radiator cap, as well as
one mounted in front of the radiator.*

The Norwegian royal family preferred the Belgian Minerva.
Like contemporary Daimlers, Minervas featured the
Knight sleeve-valve engine, only they tended to be
faster and more sporting than their British counterparts.
Here King Haakon himself sits at the wheel of an open tourer,
probably a 38 horse-power four of the 1913–4 period.

One of the most enigmatic monarchs of recent times,
the Emperor Franz Joseph of Austria,
seen sitting in a Mercedes
on a hunting excursion to the 'Walster'—
a valley in Upper Austria.

One of the most intriguing pictures in the whole collection.
The monarch is the Kaiser, the car a Mercedes Knight, the year 1913; but what is going on?
The foreign minister enquiring whether it would be all right to start the war tomorrow,
or should he wait till August 1914? The maître d'hôtel enquiring as to the
royal pleasure for tonight's dinner? Alas, we shall never know.

The Emperor Charles I in an unknown car in the Tyrol at Innsbruck.

George V in 1910 in the back of an open Daimler.
The scene is the entrance to a pier; civic and educational dignitaries abound;
but no clue is left as to the location. The car is one of Daimler's
smaller sleeve-valve types, possibly a 20 horse-power four.
The 'official' royal limousines were vast sixes rated at 57 horse-power.

1911 *and two Daimlers stand outside York Cottage, Sandringham,*
with the Prince of Wales at the wheel of the first.
In the foreground, a smallish four-cylinder tourer with Knight engine.
The big limousine is one of the earlier chain-drivers,
dating from circa 1908.

The wedding of Prince and Princess Arthur of Connaught:
the royal family at Portman Square, 15 October 1913.
The car is a four-cylinder Daimler.

The High, Oxford, 1913.
The Duke of Windsor when Prince of Wales wrote to his father,
George V, saying: 'I thought it would be much less expensive if I got one now,
though of course I would not do so without your permission'.
Permission was reluctantly granted and a 38 horse-power
touring model Daimler, painted blue and upholstered in blue leather,
was duly delivered. It was kept at the Morris garage and looked after
by William Morris, later Lord Nuffield.

*When they were away from home the British royal family
often found themselves without their familiar Daimlers.
Here at Nagpur in India on 9 January 1912
they used a Siddeley-Deasy, noted for the
dashboard radiator, curious coffin-shaped bonnet,
and a sleeve-valve engine made by Daimler.
The 1919 merger of Armstrong-Whitworth and
Siddeley-Deasy resulted in the
Armstrong-Siddeley car.*

George V leaves Goodwood House to open
the West Sussex Hospital in Chichester in 1913.
Although it did move (slowly) with the times,
the broad design of the royal Daimler
was by now established for the next
twenty-five years or so.

Faithful as ever to the Daimler, Queen Mary 'and others'
watch manoeuvres in Northamptonshire in 1913.
In those days the roof served as a grandstand
only for gentlemen. However it looks as if Her Majesty
is standing on the back seat—an activity
one would have expected her to frown upon.

On the other side of the North Sea,
the Kaiser on manoeuvres in 1910 changes from car to horse.

Somewhat public, these military operations in Germany,
for despite the big fingers on little maps to the right of the car,
the admiring civilians have fairly free access to the left.
The car is a Mercedes.

16542

A man whose country was perhaps to suffer most in the forthcoming folly.
King Albert of the Belgians at the wheel of his Excelsior circa 1922
Once considered a serious rival to Minerva, the Excelsior luxury car
usually had a six-cylinder engine (always after 1918) and was an early
convert to four-wheel brakes. Production ended in 1929, though cars
were being sold off as late as 1931.

Franz Ferdinand and his wife at Sarajevo
shortly before their assassination in 1914.
They are at this moment in a carriage and not
in the Gräf & Stift in which they were killed.

Grand Duke Michael of Russia, the country's last
Czar, who ruled only for a day in 1917, having been
banished before the war because of his morganatic marriage,
seen here in a Rolls-Royce Silver Ghost during the time
he lived in England.

_____

So it's off to war we go—
the Kaiser on the way to the Front
with his brother 'Prince Benz', i.e. Prince Henry,
whose motoring interests had shortly before this
brought him to Great Britain.

All smiles and flowers, the Kaiser reviews his troops from a Benz.
The model is not known, but in 1914 there was a choice of heavy metal—
either the 8·4-litre 33/75 or the 39/100—both with four cylinders.

George V at Vimy Ridge.
A hard journey across the Flanders mud,
but the 25 horse-power Vauxhall made it all right.

On the other side,
King George V reviews the Highland Division
from a Vauxhall. Although many different makes of car
were pressed into use during the war, it was from Vauxhall
that most of the 'staff cars' came.
Behind this one comes a Sunbeam limousine;
and in the best wartime tradition the place is not named.
Both the D-type Vauxhall and the 16 horse-power Sunbeam
remained in production for the Army throughout the war years,
though the latter firm's aero-engine contracts
meant that wartime manufacture had to be
farmed out to Rover.

*In less exacting circumstances a Rolls-Royce Landaulette,
probably one of the many lent or given by their owners
for war service, is seen providing Queen Mary (in the doorway)
with transport for a royal visit.*

---

*The Prince of Wales and George V amid an abundance of royal standards.
The car is one of those indestructible 40–50 horse-power Silver Ghosts
made from 1907 to 1925. Royalty was by now on the road in force,
but everyone was wondering what kind of road it would be
when the troubles were finally over.*

Part Two

The New Freedom

1918–1945

With the uncomfortable peace at the end of the First World War came profound changes in the social order. As far as motoring was concerned all those who had served in the forces, and many who had not, had seen the motor-car at work in a way which had not been dreamed of before the horror started. Men came home from the front to a world in which the car was to be accessible to almost everyone, instead of only the privileged. Cars began to be mass-produced, and to cost less.

Just as every common-born young man now aspired to possess his own motor-car, so the young princes of the post-war world longed for their own cars to give them an independence and a degree of privacy they could never have enjoyed in the more formal pre-war days. The Prince of Wales, for example, was most anxious to have a car like his fellow students at Oxford, and he wrote to his father, George V, to ask permission. He received a long reply from the King begging him to be careful, telling him that he did not really approve of his 'driving a motor', but giving way to him on the grounds that he claimed it as a great pleasure. He warned his son that he could not drive as well as an expert 'who does it every day of his life' and finally reminded him that if he had an accident it would 'be exaggerated in every paper in Europe'. But the Prince got his Daimler.

The Prince's brothers also took an interest in motoring, the Duke of Kent being a real enthusiast and having, among other cars, an eight-litre Bentley. The Duke of York, later to be King George VI, had 'a little sports car' of unnamed make at the time he was wooing Lady Elizabeth Bowes-Lyon; but also in his time owned several less usual cars such as a Lancia Kappa and an Aster. Even before the Daimler company had acquired the Lanchester concern there were a number of Lanchesters in royal use; and of course as more and more makes of car sprang up royalty was liable to be seen on the road in all manner of more obscure machines.

The Prince of Wales, a keen driver himself, is often seen on the ensuing pages as a passenger—and not by any means always in Daimlers. Although the Daimler was by then well established as the royal car, it was not always practical to send one on in advance of the royal party for use in the provinces, and the Prince of Wales in particular is often seen in whatever cars the local authority provided. Despite the disadvantages of the old-fashioned open tourers in wet weather, the photographs show that they provided the public with a far better view of royalty than do the present-day enclosed saloons. In this respect cars contributed to the popularity of royal families, by displaying them, and making them seem accessible to more and more of their subjects.

George V, the 'Sailor King', did not share his father's or his sons' enthusiasm for motoring, though he was well aware of the uses of the car. One day, for example, during the General Strike of 1926 when he found himself at Balmoral with an urgent need to be back in his capital, he made the five hundred mile journey by car without fuss, and was in London the following day. He realized too the economic importance of the motor industry: during the slump in the thirties he ordered five new Daimlers to keep things moving in Coventry.

Queen Mary was one of the most unlikely and most enthusiastic of motorists. She never, as far as anyone knows, drove a car—though she had been photographed at the wheel while still Princess of Wales; but she did clearly enjoy motoring—much more than the King, it would seem. There can have been few royal ladies who more neatly filled W. S. Gilbert's description of 'a right-down, regular, Royal Queen'; and yet she had a great sense of fun. She seems to have delighted in unusual forms of transport—as when she rode, for example, at the Wembley Exhibition on the so-called 'raildock', built with a chassis more usually used for corporation dust-carts! The photographs reveal her evident pleasure when out with the Army in the new-fangled Citroen Kégresse—a half-tracked vehicle developed by the former manager of Czar Nicholas II's garage; and even on a visit to the coachbuilders she seems more entertained than almost anyone else in the picture. Since she used her car so frequently the mathematical chances of her having an accident were higher than those of the rest of the royal family. When it did happen she survived it with great aplomb, and was served on the spot with a cup of tea from loyal and loving citizens.

Cars played a dramatic part in the unhappy business of Edward VIII's abdication. One day in 1936 two large black Buicks—similar but not identical models—were delivered from the showrooms at Buick House in Albemarle Street, the one to a Mr Ernest Aldrich Simpson, the other to the order of Edward Albert Christian

George Andrew Patrick David Windsor. When Mrs Simpson finally left the country, thinking she was also leaving the King, she went in her Buick, and its sleek black form was pursued by the world's journalists half way across Europe. The King's car, which was similarly pursued, was used as a decoy as he too left the country.

These Buicks, made in Canada, were the first North American cars in the British royal fleet; and they were perhaps a sign of Mrs Simpson's influence. However it is true that David Dunbar Buick was a Scotsman, who was famous for the manufacture of enamel bathtubs before he went to America and turned his mind to the motor business.

In other parts of Europe American cars were much favoured by the royal houses—especially in countries which had no domestic industry. Of course in the late twenties and thirties the better American cars offered a great deal of space and comfort for a rather more modest outlay than the acknowledged masters such as Rolls-Royce and Mercedes-Benz. On the whole, however, local loyalties held sway, and if the national manufacturer did not make a suitably large car, special efforts were made to create something suitable.

Among the more exotic royal cars—as can be seen from the picture on page 115—was the Isotta Fraschini given to the Empress of Ethiopia by the King of Italy. The most gaudy, perhaps, were those made for the princes of India. Bright orange was their favourite choice, with lots and lots of chromium plate (once polished brass had gone out of fashion). But the most royal of royal cars was the Bugatti 'Royale'. Only six were made—and none of them in the end went to royalty, though King Carol of Rumania was said to have ordered one. When the cars were finished the cost was so prodigious that no monarchs could afford them.

While the British royal family was always discouraged from motor-racing as a hobby, certain foreign princes continued in the twenties and thirties to excel in this field. Prince Nicholas of Rumania drove a Duesenberg at Le Mans in 1935, and participated in many races in his own country in a variety of cars, some of which look a bit as if they were run up in the royal mews. The German Prince zu Leiningen drove one of the Auto-Union Grand Prix cars as part of the team in its earliest days, and then made some appearances with a British E.R.A. But the most famous of royal motor racers was 'B. Bira'. H.H. Prince Bira Birabongse of Siam had been educated in England and during his university days had begun to take an interest in motor-racing. In the mid-thirties he and his cousin, H.R.H. Prince Chula Chakrabongse, formed a highly professional 'stable' called 'The White Mouse'. With his two E.R.A.'s called Romulus and Remus, B. Bira achieved a notable series of successes.

As the Second World War approached motoring, save for military purposes, was abandoned. But this was the time when Princess Elizabeth became a fully fledged motorist. 'Driving and Maintenance' was an important part of her Junior Officer's course in the ATS, and the press chose this as the best way of showing the public that the future queen was doing her bit.

The Prince of Wales achieved enormous popularity after the First World War.
The world's most eligible bachelor, he combined a handsome figure and a lively mind
with the kind of zest that makes a young man get up to leave the car
before it had finally come to a halt. Here he is in the back seat of a Hudson in Perth,
Western Australia in 1920. This big Super Six had a long run (1916–29,
in various forms) and was well loved in the Antipodes.

*A Lanchester in 1923—long before the Lanchester company became part of the Daimler concern.
This model would be a Forty with 6·2-litre overhead-camshaft six-cylinder engine,
as current throughout the 1920s. The passenger is, of course, the Prince of Wales again,
this time in the Midlands.*

The Prince of Wales in a Crossley: Hull, 1926.
Although they never achieved the status of official royal cars, Crossleys were often used on royal occasions.
This one was among the company's first six-cylinder models, a 2·7-litre 18/50.
Capacity went up to 3·2 litres during 1927, and the model survived in
various forms to the end of private-car production at Crossley in 1937.
Behind the Crossley is a Daimler—probably a civic car since
by this time the royal models had black radiators.

*The Prince at the wheel of a Willys-Knight
tourer during a visit to the factory in 1920 or 1921.
Beside him is Major Crossley, sales director of Willys-Overland-Crossley,
the American company which built the make for the British market.
The left-hand steering, however, suggests that this one
was built entirely in America.*

The Duke of Kent ranked high among royal enthusiasts between the wars.
Here is one of his early cars, a 3-litre Bentley.
Announced in 1919, this model, Bentley's first, had a ten-year run,
and won the Le Mans 24-hour race in 1924 and 1927.

And here his 8-litre model.
This was later requisitioned by the Armed Forces in World War II, and still exists,
albeit with a different body. The magnificent 8-litres were almost the last produced
by Bentley before it was bought by Rolls-Royce in 1931; *but the photograph must date*
from somewhat later because the car behind is a Wolseley Hornet Special,
which did not come on to the market until 1932.

King Alfonso of Spain's long-standing love of cars continued unabated.
The original caption on this picture claims that it shows
'Alfonso XIII in his first 32CV Hispano-Suiza Type 41'. It is dated 1919.
Type 41 was the Spanish-built edition of this model,
usually associated with the French factory at Bois-Colombes
and current until about 1930, though later 8-litre derivatives were still being
made at Barcelona at the outbreak of the Civil War in 1936.

A rather less formal shot of His Majesty in a similar, but certainly not the same, car.
Probably in the early twenties.

A well-posed picture of Queen Victoria Eugenie of Spain
with an Austin Twenty 'Ranelagh' limousine outside Kensington Palace in 1931.
The six-cylinder twenty (1927–38) had a successful career as a mayoral and executive carriage,
though it seldom figured in royal circles.

The German Crown Prince, by now in exile, kept up his interest in motor cars—
notably in Mercedes-Benz models like the one with which he is seen here.
This is one of the company's first supercharged sixes, a 24/100/140
(33/140 in England) of circa 1924.

Prince Harald of Denmark—
the younger brother of the much-loved King Christian X,
with Princess Caroline Mathilde sitting on the running board beside him.
The time must be the twenties and the American car looks like
a Chandler, ancestor of today's Pontiac.

———————————

An early picture of Crown Prince Frederick of Denmark, who
became a keen motorist in later years, when he was King Frederick IX.
The car is a Scripps-Booth, a forgotten American light car of World War I vintage.
Some of these had miniature V8 engines made by the Ferro company.

———————————

The Duke and Duchess of York getting into a Crossley at Brighton.
Once again it is a big six, now with the 3.2-litre engine.
The seven-seater limousine version was called a 'Canberra',
to commemorate the model's use on royal tours in Australia.

Queen Mary suddenly emerges as a much more adventurous motorist than one would have expected.
Here she is at the Wembley exhibition, with the King beside her in what was called the 'raildock'—
built on a chassis which had several commercial uses, but was unusually adapted here for passengers.
It was complementary to the never-stop-railway as a means of exhibition transport.

Obviously enjoying herself hugely, here is Queen Mary with the Army,
both of them playing with a new toy. The vehicle is a Citroen Kégresse—
a half-tracked car which had just achieved some fame for having made
the first successful crossing of the Sahara Desert.
There were larger, strictly military, models; but this was an adaptation
of one of the company's private cars. M. Kégresse, who invented the device,
had been at one time the manager of Czar Nicholas II's garage in Russia.
Note the auxiliary cooling surfaces on the bonnet top.
The date of this car is 1922–3, which makes the base model either a
1·3-litre Type A or the Type B which replaced it.

This is 1927 and the second day of the Ascot meeting:
the royal party changes from motor cars to semi-state coaches before arriving on the course.
The big royal Daimlers of this period were Knight-engined 57 horse-power sixes:
the first double-sixes did not enter royal service until 1928, though
two 57s were re-engined with twelve-cylinder units in 1932.

Buckler's Hard, 10 August 1928.
Queen Mary had been brought over from Cowes, while George V
had gone racing in Britannia and landed at Buckler's Hard from John Montagu's Cygnet.
The Queen was then driven in the Rolls-Royce—an early 40/50 horse-power
Phantom I, shown here—to tea at Palace House.

The car is unidentified but the occasion merited much comment.
It was 29 September 1929, and the first royal visit to Eastbourne
since Edward VII had been there more than twenty-five years previously.
It was a brief visit but the Duke and Duchess of York drove through crowded streets in an open car.

This Landaulette, with coachwork by Cesare Sala, was built on
the Isotta Fraschini type 8A chassis to the order of the King of Italy
as a gift to Zauditu, Empress of Ethiopia, in 1927.
The big straight-eight Isotta Fraschini was announced in 1919
and remained in production until 1934–5.

Queen Elizabeth of the Belgians in goggles and headscarf
after an obviously thrilling run in a racing car
during her visit to the Fiat factory in 1924.
The man with the flowers is her husband, King Albert,
and the car one of Fiat's 2-litre eight-cylinder Grand Prix machines.

———————————————

Prince Leopold of the Belgians, then the Duke of Brabant,
with Princess Astrid, who was later tragically killed
in a motor accident in Switzerland in 1935.
The car appears to be a Minerva.

One of several American cars used by Prince Wilhelm of Sweden—
a 1927 Model 264 Nash, presented to him by the Scandinavian employees
of Nash Motors Company, Kenosha, Wisconsin.
The lady is not named.

Prince Olaf of Norway driving a Fiat 501 some time in the twenties.
This popular 1·5-litre model was noted for its smoothness
and silence and was on the market from 1919 to 1926.
The royal one carries standard roadster bodywork,
though the bumpers were an extra.

Queen Maud of Norway with a big Sunbeam limousine in about 1930.
The car is a little earlier than that, probably a six-cylinder 25.
Straight-eight models almost invariably wore vee radiators.

Queen Marie of Rumania with her sister the Princess of Hohenlohe-Langenberg.
The car is an American Lincoln with V8 engine, styling suggesting the mid-twenties.
Though created by Henry M. Leland of Cadillac fame, Lincoln came under Ford control in 1922.

Prince Michael of Rumania in 1936. He was to be another royal enthusiast
and this must have been one of his earliest experiences as a motorist.
The picture was taken on the island of Brioni, which is now part of Yugoslavia.
The car is a Fiat 'Topolino' (Mickey Mouse), one of the best baby cars of the later thirties.
The model was in production for nineteen years from 1936.

1933: the Princess Mother of Rumania looks out from the otherwise shrouded back seat of a Lancia somewhere in England. The car is interesting because the coachwork is by the Italian firm of Pinin Farina (the sign is just visible above the toolbox on the front wing). When Pinin Farina set up on his own in Turin in 1930, one of his first commissions was to build a Lancia for the Queen of Rumania which looked almost exactly similar to this car. Whether this is it, or another like it from the same source, we cannot say.

It is difficult to know if the Vicars of Christ should be included among royalty or not
—not that any of them has ever publicly evinced enthusiasm for motor cars.
Here is Pius XI in 1929 with a Type 525 Fiat saloon which the manufacturers had just given him.
Beside him, with white hair, is Senator Agnelli, whose family still rule Fiat
to this day, almost like royalty themselves. The 525 was their prestige model,
but in a time of depression, a modest 3·7 litres of engine sufficed.

This picture was taken at a wedding in Jodhpur on 24 April 1932.
It shows the Maharaja of Jaipur (the bridegroom)
getting ready to go (by Rolls-Royce) to the bride's house.

Queen Elizabeth, the Queen Mother (then the Duchess of York)
with Mrs 'Bill' Wisdom at Brooklands.
Mrs Wisdom was one of that track's most famous
and successful drivers in the years before the war,
and is here seen in a 4·5-litre Invicta—
the low-chassis 4·5-litre '100 m.p.h.' model of 1931–5.

The most famous of motor-sporting princes was 'B. Bira',
a pseudonym which concealed the identity of Prince Birabongse of Siam. He ran a very successful stable of
British E.R.A. racing cars in the years before the World War II, presided over by his cousin Prince Chula Chakrabongse.
He was still racing after the war, but independently. He is seen here at Crystal Palace Circuit in 1937,
receiving the winner's cup for the first London Grand Prix from the famous motor dealer Charles Follett.
Facing the camera in a cap is Prince Chula.

*One of the keenest of royal racing drivers was Prince Nicholas of Rumania.
In this mysterious photograph the Prince's car is thought by the sender
to be a Duesenberg Special, and it is sideways-on in front of a Bugatti;
but beyond that we know nothing.*

*Prince Nicholas drove a Duesenberg at Le Mans in 1935
and is here seen in one of the Pescara 24-hour races
in an Alfa Romeo he shared with Mario Tadini. They managed to finish third overall.
The car is the six-cylinder 2·3-litre model as made from 1934 to 1939 —
probably an early version without independent suspension.*

While some royals were racing, others preferred the thrills
of the African bush. On this occasion, the Duke of Kent
has just got out of the royal Humber to watch the ferry land.
It was in circumstances like this that Billy Rootes came into his own.
This model is a Pullman of the 1934–5 run with a 3·5-litre engine.
The model was around for nearly a quarter of a century (1930–54)
and was marketed under the apt slogan, 'The Ambassador of Cars'.
The royal Daimlers would have been unsuitable for
an African trip anyway, and whenever the need arose
Billy always had one of his Humbers ready.

Queen Maud of Norway is seen here at Sandringham in April 1936:
a 4·1-litre Humber this time with independently sprung front wheels.

Rootes (on the right with a rather pensive expression)
from time to time provided other royal transport.
This is the Prince of Wales at the Humber works in 1934
trying out his grandfather's tricycle.

The demands of protocol and tradition come into open conflict in this happy picture of Queen Juliana
of the Netherlands and her husband Prince Bernhard on a tandem at the time of their engagement.
Cycling in Holland is a national institution; and what could be more natural than that
royalty should travel in the same way as everyone else? However, upon closer inspection
is not the same way as everyone else: for 'Daisy' is on the front seat of the bicycle
made for two (as indeed a Queen should be) and however sweet she may look
it is upon the rear seat that the lady is normally to be found.
Feelings ran high at the time as to whether loyalty to the crown
or loyalty to tradition should take precedence.

*No argument was necessary here, however: Prince Bernhard is clearly
in command at the wheel of a mid-thirties Ford V8 as the royal pair wait,
just like everyone else, at a Dutch level crossing.*

Another bevy of Luxembourgers.
From left to right
the Grand Duchess Charlotte, Princess Marie-Adelaide,
Princess Elizabeth, Prince Felix,
Princess Maria-Gabrielle and Prince Jean.
The gentleman at the wheel
of the Chrysler is unnamed.
The car would be one of the smaller
Imperial Eights of 1932–3.

Cars enabled subjects to see their monarchs—especially when, as Queen Mary
always did, they sat not in the back seat but further forward in the car.
This is incidentally a typical royal Daimler—Her Majesty's own OHV 'double six';
and as it is not the King's car it carries a number plate.
The OHV twelve-cylinders were made to special order only between 1935 and 1938.

Cars also provided a chance for a loving public to see the royal children.
Princess Margaret and Princess Elizabeth with their mother.

A royal Daimler in the East End of London
during the Silver Jubilee celebrations on 12 May 1935.
The shape of the front wings suggests that this
particular car had been in royal service for some time:
it looks like one of the sleeve-valve double sixes
acquired in 1932.

Every middle-aged person's idea of royal motoring:
George VI and his family leave the Thistle Ceremony
at St Giles Cathedral, Edinburgh, in 1937
in one of the high Hooper-bodied straight-eight
Daimlers that then constituted the royal fleet.
By tradition the cars had black radiators,
very little chromium, and were finished, as indeed
are the royal cars today, in dark red and black.
The folding head of those landaulettes which allowed
the public an excellent view of their Majesties
has today of course been replaced by large
expanses of glass and plastic.

This interesting Sunbeam is a 1934 car built for the Duke of Gloucester on the 25 horse-power long chassis. It was subsequently re-bodied by Thrupp and Maberly as a six-light limousine.

*The Duke had a Rolls-Royce for his personal use, which had his own
personal mascot on it instead of the more usual 'Silver Lady'.*

My Car after the
23rd J...

Nothing can really be added to Queen Mary's own caption.
Accidents do happen even when royalty are on the road.
It was in West London and the other vehicle involved was a lorry.
The car went over on its side. Having emerged unscathed,
Queen Mary took a cup of tea in a neighbouring house
and then continued her journey in another car.

*Comparatively unaffected by the threat of war, Their Royal Highnesses
Prince Gustaf and Princess Sibylla of Sweden with their Horch—
one of the complicated range of single overhead-camshaft straight-eights
produced between 1931 and the outbreak of World War II. They came as anything
from a sporting cabriolet to a formal limousine like this one.*

The Crown Prince of Norway again,
this time with his family and a straight-eight Buick,
either a 50 or 60 series of 1934–5.

Norges Kronprinsfamilie.

War. The King and Queen in a Wolseley with Sir John Anderson
touring the ARP centres in South East London.
The King was wearing the uniform of a Marshall of the R.A.F.
This car was probably an 18–80 horse-power model as favoured by
police forces in those days, though the optional 'De Ville' body
suggests that it was not actually a police car.

Princess Elizabeth was determined during the war to do what other girls were doing.
Having overcome her father's resistance she went on a Junior Officer's course which included
Motor Transport training. The photographs have a rather posed appearance
but she herself took the job very seriously.

Even in Sweden, where there was no war, there were problems.
The Swedish king, looking very grim, enters his 1931 royal Cadillac.
The second picture shows a later model with a charcoal-gas generator.

Part Three

Recent Years

1945–1980

By the end of the Second World War it was some fifty years since the birth of the motor-car and the death of Queen Victoria. Both cars and royalty had changed beyond recognition. Colonies were out of fashion, and crowned heads—like new cars—were in short supply. It was a long way from the time when Jakob Lohner, coachbuilder to His Royal and Imperial Majesty Franz Joseph of Austria, had decided that noisy smelly automobiles were too vulgar for his customers and that they ought to use electric cars. A long way, too, from George V's admonition to the Prince of Wales about careful driving and the difficulties that would arise if he were involved in any accident, however slight. For in the post-war years royalty came a great deal nearer their people. The British royal family did not go as far as that of, say, Denmark or Holland, where one might bump into the Queen in a department store; but nevertheless they began to feel free to drive themselves where they liked in whatever cars they liked.

Shortly after the war a little MG Midget began to be seen entering the gates of Buckingham Palace at frequent intervals. It was not at all the kind of car that the public associated with royalty, and it appeared to be driven by a young naval officer. He is said to have made the journey from his station in Corsham in such an alarmingly short time that the Queen expressed the hope that he wouldn't kill himself coming to see her daughter. The young man was of course the Duke of Edinburgh.

Without being a motoring fanatic the Duke of Edinburgh had a proper young man's interest in cars. With the new-found freedom of modern royalty he would even hire a car when necessary. He did this once in Australia and caused some diplomatic difficulty by signing the hiring form 'Philip'. This was not good enough for the garage, who had never come across such a name before: so he then added 'of Greece', which did not immediately solve the problem.

In later years, as the Queen's husband, the Prince was often seen at the wheel of his own three-litre Lagonda drop-head coupé, and this was followed by a not dissimilar Alvis. It is also on record that he was lent for a time a very special car from Rolls-Royce, with the then-new eight-cylinder engine. It was known, for obvious reasons, as 'the Scalded Cat'. The story goes that he was reluctant to part with it, and needed a good deal of persuading that as it was an experimental model the makers rather wanted it back!

In their early years together both he and the young Queen were often seen driving their own cars, the Queen herself in a three-litre Rover as well as a specially commissioned Daimler with a Hooper Empress body. On her country estates she generally chooses to drive a sturdy Land-Rover. It would probably be wrong to suggest that Her Majesty has any great love of motor-cars, but she clearly understands them and is at ease in them on both public and private occasions.

British royal patronage has switched in post-war years from Daimler to Rolls-Royce. The Rolls had been a royal car for many years outside Great Britain, and the company was alone in producing a model which it would supply only to heads of state: the Phantom IV. This is now out of production, but there is one in the British royal stable, and an even more interesting version (which must have been a close relative of 'the Scalded Cat') was built for the former Shah of Iran.

In the early days of the 'Mini' it was rendered classless by being the chosen car of Princess Margaret and the Earl of Snowdon; all sorts of people were happy to 'keep up with the Armstrong-Joneses'. Cars were now a common denominator, and the cars that royalty drove in private enabled them to be like everyone else.

Now that the present Queen's family has grown up to motoring, royalty can be found on any road in Britain driving themselves from place to place in the same way as ordinary mortals—and suffering the same slings and arrows. The police do not always pursue royalty as they would the rest of us; but Princess Anne at least has been 'done' for speeding. Imagination boggles at the thought of some hapless Balmoral bobby trying to apprehend Queen Victoria for a misdemeanour with her dog-cart.

Given this new freedom a number of modern royals have taken to the road with a vengeance. Prince Bertil of Sweden and Prince Bernhard of the Netherlands have become Ferrari fans; and King Michael of Rumania, both before and after his exile, has been an authority on, and great enthusiast for, Jeeps. A number of the younger members of the British royal family have even become competition minded: Prince Michael of Kent has driven in two R.A.C. rallies as well as the World Cup Rally to Mexico; both he and his brother the Duke of Kent have taken the high speed course organized by the British School of Motoring. Prince Michael is now President of the R.A.C., and the Duke of Kent President of the A.A.

The post-war era has brought drastic changes in the motor industry which have affected both royalty and commoners on the road. The imposition in Britain of a dizzy 'purchase tax' on cars made the expensive models almost prohibitive. Many of the famous firms of coachbuilders went under as a result of this tax, and though the rich, and royalty among them, were able to support the dying industry for a few years, the struggle was in vain. Apart from questions of cost the spate of regulations which nowadays govern the construction of a motor car render it virtually impossible to build a 'one-off' model, and Sergio Pininfarina now reckons that if he were to try to build an individual car the cost would be in excess of £100,000.

Motoring changed almost overnight in the mid-sixties when Ralph Nader, an American lawyer, published his book *Unsafe at Any Speed*. The world suddenly became safety conscious; seat belts, speed limits, crash tests proliferated. Europe followed America with slavish admiration, and not even crowned heads escaped; indeed it became an essential function of royalty to become 'patrons' of this or that worthy preventative society. The unfortunate Duke of Edinburgh had one of his very rare minor scrapes with another car only just after he had delivered an eloquent speech on road safety.

Then came two more important developments which greatly altered the state of affairs on the roads: a series of oil crises; and the invasion of both the European and American markets by the Japanese. Even the makers of royal cars had a rough time of it. Daimler became part of Jaguar, and although the big limousine has hung on to a share of the diminishing market it is no royal car in the sense that the old Daimlers were. Sir William Rootes, who so often supplied royal cars in the outposts of Empire, had to sell out to Chrysler, who have now had to sell out to Peugeot, who have decided to revive the name Talbot, which brings them back to English nobility if not to royalty.

Rolls-Royce under the pressure of developing jet aero-engines went to the financial wall; but Rolls-Royce Motors rose, phoenix-like, from the flames and continue to produce their royal models. Among the other cars now patronized by royalty the new Lagonda is as much coveted by princes as by paupers, and the Range-Rover and its fellow Land-Rover continue to have special royal connotations.

Nevertheless, as the turn of the century approaches, it is clear that motoring as we have known it in the past is unlikely to continue, and the days of royalty—or indeed any of us—on the road may well be numbered. The splendours of the royal train, now rarely seen, may soon be due for a fascinating revival.

*Victory celebrations usually involved royalty remaining in one spot while the celebration rolled past them;
but at the return of the 'free' Norwegian army on 13 May 1945 Crown Prince Olaf sat up high on the back
of his Buick, regardless of the danger of assassination, to acknowledge his people's happy cheers.
The car is, of course, of pre-war manufacture; it looks like a 1937 or 1938 model
with factory-built convertible sedan bodywork.*

Meanwhile, hailed as the architect of a victory, a 'Former Naval Person' who never quite achieved royal status drove through the streets of Oslo in King Haakon's car. With him in the centre is Mrs Churchill. This is the later version of Mercedes-Benz' supercharged 7·7-litre Grosser with parade cabriolet bodywork, a three-tonner but still capable of 105 m.p.h. Much favoured by Nazi bigwigs, it was also used by other heads of state, among them Portugal's President Salazar.

On the whole motoring after the war went back to where it had been before.
Daimler produced a new six-cylinder model using the engine they had developed for their armoured car.
This one, a 4·1-litre DE27, was a wedding gift to Princess Elizabeth from the RAF and WAAF:
it was delivered to Buckingham Palace on the morning of 2 February 1948.
Its companion straight-eight was recognized royal wear in the early post-war years.

During a visit to the Vauxhall works His Royal Highness the Duke of Edinburgh took the wheel of a Vauxhall VX4/90—one of the company's more sporting models. This one dates from the early seventies, though the first cars to bear the name came out in 1963.

The Queen, too, had taken to the steering wheel. Her car, in this picture,
is a Daimler, and one made for her with the now celebrated Hooper 'Empress Line' body.
No date, but the children give the game away.

A picture taken in Windsor Great Park in 1968.
Prince Andrew is a passenger. The car is a Vauxhall Cresta estate of the type announced for 1960
and marketed in this shape for several years thereafter.

Royal Daimlers persisted, even in India. Here—Bangalore, 1961—
is the eight-cylinder model again with a special open body suitable to the occasion.
By this time the early post-war straight-eights were getting long in the tooth.
The last one had been delivered in 1953. The Queen is accompanied by
the Governor of the State of Mysore.

*Meanwhile the Duke of Edinburgh travelled in another car —
a Canadian Dodge 'Mayfair' of 1954. The car is in fact a Plymouth
with Dodge badging specially produced for the Canadian market.*

In New Delhi, on the same tour,
The Queen used a Mercedes, one of those
six-cylinder 300 parade cabriolets
of the mid-fifties so beloved of
heads of emergent republics.
Otherwise American products seem
to have won the day.

Her Majesty the Queen in a Land Rover in Aden
during the Commonwealth tour of 1953, *just after her coronation.*

King Michael of Rumania preferred the American equivalent, the Jeep.
This is a shot from 1943, with his sister, whose only comment was
that the vehicles were 'bloody uncomfortable'.

A rather special Rolls-Royce.
This is the celebrated Phantom IV
which was only available to heads of state.
It had the eight-cylinder engine
used in the 'Scalded Cat' (to which
the Duke of Edinburgh became so attached).
In this case the coachwork is, as usual,
by Hooper, but by now (1949) the day of
the royal Daimlers was ended.

Not all royal cars have been grand cars. This is a Triumph Renown, much
the same as anyone could buy, delivered for the use of the Duke of Gloucester.
The highly successful body shape of these Triumphs was inspired by a design
from before the war, built in very small numbers by Freestone & Webb.
The Renown itself ran from 1950 to 1954, and used the same
mechanical elements as the Standard Vanguard.

———————————

The Prince and Princess of Monaco after their wedding—in a Rolls-Royce
which was a present to them from the people of the principality.

———————————

Some rather modest royal vehicles.
Prince William of Gloucester on 16 June 1944
at Barnwell Manor, Peterborough.

Their Royal Highnesses Prince Charles and Princess Anne, at Balmoral on 20 September 1952.

*High drama lurks behind this happy photograph, taken in 1950, of King Leopold of the Belgians
helping Prince Alexander, his son by his second wife, the Princess de Rethy, with his model Bugatti.
Behind stands the heir apparent, Prince Baudouin, soon to become King.
When this picture was taken Belgium was divided over Leopold's surrender to the Germans at the start of the war:
the royal family was living at Pregny on the shores of
Lake Geneva in Switzerland, awaiting the decision of the Belgian people.
Strangely the model car, one of Bugatti's own creations and now much sought after
as a collector's piece (and surely one of the most expensive toys ever),
was described in the contemporary caption as 'The Family Flivver—
used by all the children'.*

*A much happier tale is told by this picture of the Duke of Kent's son Nicholas
in the model of the Grand Prix Sunbeam presented to the Duke by the Trustees
on the occasion of the opening of the National Motor Museum at Beaulieu.*

King Leopold with his own Ferrari, and the Princess de Rethy.

1967: Princess Paola, the Princess of Liège, obviously enjoying herself at the Alfa Romeo works in Milan.

179

Another Royal in the cockpit of a racing car, the Duke of Kent.
On 27 April 1959 he visited Charterhall racing circuit in Scotland,
where J. G. McBain gave him a spin at speeds approaching 150 m.p.h.,
before he took over the wheel himself.

This Aston Martin DB2/4 was the young Duke of Kent's
third car. With a 3-litre twin-overhead-camshaft engine
based on W. O. Bentley's 1946 Lagonda design,
the DB 2/4 was capable of 115 m.p.h.
The photograph dates from around 1955.

Among the world's most popular sports cars—
the Porsche. This one appears with its royal owner,
H.R.H. Prince Wilhelm of Sweden.
The classical 356 shape was current from 1949 to 1965.

———————————

Prince Bertil of Sweden,
a very sporting motorist, lent his support to Vintage events.
Here he is on a rally in his type
38/44 Bugatti roadster of late 1920s vintage.

———————————

Even royal drivers have been known to come off the road.
This corner outside Stockholm is known as
'the King's Curve' ever since this accident happened.
Neither King nor Cadillac—one of the seven-seater
Model-75s made in 1939—was much damaged.

The late Shah of Iran had a number of exciting cars
besides the Phantom IV we have already seen,
and was, no doubt, planning the acquisition
of another when this photograph was taken.
He is shown in conversation with Enzo Ferrari (on the right).

*Sergio Pininfarina, son of the founder of the firm,
and now in charge of it, talks to Prince Bernhard of the Netherlands
with Enzo Ferrari, in dark glasses, in the background.*

These younger members of the royal family found the universal and classless Mini ideal for London motoring. Prince Michael of Kent is shown at the wheel on the very day he 'passed out' from Sandhurst. Princess Alexandra is in the back seat, and about to join them is the Duchess of Kent.

The Duke of Kent at the wheel of a Rolls-Royce Corniche at a British Motor Show in the 1970s.
With him is David Plastow, managing director of Rolls-Royce Motors.

Princess Anne looking radiant at the wheel of a Rover 2000.
The 2000, introduced in 1964, had a successful twelve-year run.

This last picture suggests that the royal interest in motoring will continue.
The heir to the throne fund-raising in a vintage taxi at Buckingham Palace,
during his mother's Silver Jubilee year.